how2become

Cabin Crew Interview Questions and Answers

www.How2Become.com

Orders: Please contact How2Become Ltd, Suite 14, 50 Churchill Square Business Centre, Kings Hill, Kent ME19 4YU.

You can order through Amazon.co.uk under ISBN 9781909229013, via the website www.How2Become.com, Gardners or Bertrams.

ISBN: 9781909229013

First published 2012

Updated 2017

Copyright © 2017 Jessica Bond.

Typeset for How2Become Ltd by Gemma Butler

Disclaimer

Every effort has been made to ensure that the information contained within this guide is accurate at the time of publication. How2Become Ltd is not responsible for anyone failing any part of any selection process as a result of the information contained within this guide. How2Become Ltd and their authors cannot accept any responsibility for any errors or omissions within this guide, however caused. No responsibility for loss or damage occasioned by any person acting, or refraining from action, as a result of the material in this publication can be accepted by How2Become Ltd.

The information within this guide does not represent the views of any third-party service or organisation.

Contents

Dear Sir/Madam,

Welcome to your new guide, *Cabin Crew Interview Questions and Answers*. You will find this guide an invaluable resource in your pursuit to becoming cabin crew with any of the worldwide airlines. The information within this guide has been supplied by Jessica Bond, a serving senior cabin crew member with a major UK-based airline. She has 14 years' experience in the role and is also a member of the cabin crew training and recruitment team within the airline industry.

The guide itself has been divided up in to useful sections to help you prepare effectively. To begin with, we will provide you with details about the role of cabin crew. This is extremely important, so please don't miss out this section. If you want to pass the cabin crew interview then you MUST have a thorough understanding of what the role involves.

Once we have covered the role we will then provide you a host of sample interview questions and tips on how to best answer them.

Finally, you won't achieve much in life without hard work, commitment and dedication. Please take the time to prepare for the cabin crew selection process properly; it will be worth it!

If you need any further assistance with the selection process, please visit our award-winning website:

www.How2Become.com

Good luck and best wishes,

The how 2 become team

A Message From Jessica

Hello! My name's Jessica Bond and I'm the author of this guide. As mentioned on the previous page, I have 14 years' experience in the airline industry. So I have a huge amount of knowledge and insider tips to share, which I will do throughout this book.

The advice and interview questions that I have provided you with within this guide are some of the questions that I got asked when I first applied to become cabin crew. As well as this, you will find additional questions that I uncovered during my research, which involved talking to other experienced individuals in the industry and more.

While I cannot guarantee that they will be the exact questions that you yourself will be asked at interview, I believe that they will prove to be an invaluable resource to assist your preparation for the big day.

But, before you get started, I'd like to pass on a few important tips about the cabin crew interview that I think you should keep in mind while reading the rest of the guide.

When preparing for the interview, focus on the following key areas:

1. Learn the role inside out. You will get asked questions about the role and it is important that you have a thorough understanding of what it involves.

2. Be able to provide evidence of where you can meet the qualities of cabin crew. For example, one of the main qualities is that of customer care/service. Before you attend the interview, you should be able to give an example of where you personally carried out excellent customer service in a work-related role. If you have evidence for each key area of the role then you will be far better prepared than most candidates.

3. Learn about the airline you are applying to join. You can do this by visiting their website and finding out more about them. If you have flown with the airline previously, what did you like about them and what makes them better than their rivals? Before you attend the interview, I recommend that you find out the following facts relating to the airline:

•   What is their mission or goal?

•   What is the name of their website?

- Where do they fly to and from?

- How many people (approx.) work for the airline?

- What is their busiest route?

- What is their USP? (unique selling point). For example, some airlines pride themselves on cheaper fares, whilst others pride themselves on exceptional service and quality.

- What's happening within the company right now? Check out the 'news' section on their website.

- What is their corporate responsibility? This basically means the steps the airline is taking to protect the environment and protect the world we live in. Remember, aircraft have a huge carbon footprint and airlines have a responsibility to reduce that.

- What offers does the airline have to its members?

   Of course, there are many other areas that you could research for your interview. However, the ones that I provided you with here are the key areas I concentrated on during the preparation for my interview. Please find the list of things to focus on continued below:

4. Appearance is VERY important! Think carefully about how you intend to dress for your interview. Personal hygiene is important too. If you have reached the interview stage then you don't need me to tell you what you should be wearing; however, think about this:

   Airlines pride themselves on excellent customer service and part of this includes cabin crew dressing smart and looking the part. Spend time thinking about how you are going to dress for the interview as you will be assessed on your presentation.

5. Be confident – cabin crew are confident people. Having said that, there is a fine line between being confident and arrogant; don't step over this line! In addition, you should have a cheery disposition and smile! Try to enjoy the whole experience and don't be too nervous. If you are good, you will get selected!

Good luck!

Jessica

What Are the Assessors Looking For?

Many people ask: 'What are the assessors looking for at the interview?' A good question. The best way to go about answering it is to consider what assessors are looking for throughout the entire selection process, not just at interview. That way, you will be able to demonstrate these qualities when it does come to interview day.

See below for each key area (not in order of priority) followed by some tips on why it is important.

A Passion for The Job
Most people who apply to become cabin crew want to travel the world. This is not enough on its own. You need to be a caring person who strives to work in a customer-focused role and genuinely get a buzz out of helping people. For all the presumed glamour that comes with the role of cabin crew, you are essentially providing a service to passengers. You should also have the ability to 'step up' and take responsibility when things go wrong.

Professionalism
The airline industry is very competitive and cabin crew are the 'face' of the airline. You must be professional at all times as the airline wants its passengers to come back and travel with them time and time again. If you provide a poor service then there is no way they will come back! Being professional is also about communicating with your team members, always having a smile on your face and having an ability or desire to continually learn and develop. You should never 'back stab' or talk about other cabin crew members behind their back. Be respectful to one another and always be kind.

Image
You are essentially the face of your airline and as such, your image is crucial! You have to look the part and you will be assessed on how you present yourself at interview/assessment. As cabin crew, you will be working very long hours and you should look as fresh at the end of the flight as you do at the beginning.

Customer Service Experience
As I have already mentioned, customer service is very important. You must be able to listen to customers' complaints and questions and have an ability to resolve them quickly and successfully. You should understand how to resolve complaints, and be fully aware of your airlines procedures for delivering outstanding customer service. It is

also important that you can provide the interview panel with examples of great customer service you have yourself witnessed and delivered.

Excellent Timekeeping

If you want to lose your job, simply be late! I can assure you that if you are late for your interview you will not be successful. Airlines rely on cabin crew to be on time, every time. Your life should also be flexible enough to accommodate your rota and shifts. Timekeeping is essential to the role and it is up to you to manage your life around your working patterns and rotas.

Personal Responsibility

Of course, when working as a cabin crew you will have many daily responsibilities. Firstly, you will be required to be punctual at all times in order to keep to the airline's schedule. Secondly, your responsibilities while airborne are numerous as well, which are focused on customer safety and comfort. Of course, this requires a thorough knowledge of all training and procedures that you will have gone through.

As well as this, it is your responsibility to admit it when you make a mistake, which of course can happen when working in difficult and pressurised situations, or even emergencies. It is very important to always take responsibility for your actions.

Flexible and Adaptable

As cabin crew, things can and will change at a moment's notice. You will also have standby duties to be responsible for, just in case another member of the cabin crew team goes sick. Above all, you must have a flexible approach and attitude to work at all times.

Teamwork and Communication

These two are probably some of the most important qualities you will need as cabin crew. You should have previous experience of working as part of a team, and be able to communicate effectively with your team members as well as the passengers. At interview, make sure you have examples of where you have worked as part of a team to achieve a common goal, and also where you have communicated with others in order to achieve a task.

The Role of Cabin Crew

Members of cabin crew have two main roles in their job. These are: ensuring the safety of all the passengers and delivering great customer service.

Cabin crew must also have excellent interpersonal skills, which will be assessed throughout the selection process. As previously stated, how well you can deal with members of the public will have an enormous impact on your overall success.

Above all, however, the main focus of the role of cabin crew will always be on safety. A serious decision to evacuate the aircraft will always rest with the cockpit crew, but the cabin crew have the responsibility to oversee the evacuation and make sure that this is correctly carried out according to procedure.

The key role of cabin crew remains exactly as it always has been, and that is to keep the passengers safe. The cabin crew are obliged to provide a safety briefing before the flight and to ensure that the passengers pay attention to it. If an emergency situation arises, the cabin crew are trained to help everyone leave the aircraft swiftly and safely.

The cabin crew can make or break the reputation of an airline. They must be well-presented, be professional, and make a good impression on passengers to encourage them to use the same airline again in the future. Airline companies know that passengers who experience bad customer service from cabin crew will change the airline they use; it's as simple as that.

This is why airline companies look for future cabin crew members who go to the assessment and interview with their eyes open to what the role of cabin crew is all about. They will want them to have shown an interest in the airline they have applied to, by knowing some history about the airline and where they fly to and from. They must be people who work well in a group and that have a friendly, confident and caring nature.

Before you attend the assessments and the interview it is vital that you understand the role as well as the key qualities required to carry out the role competently. Let's take a look at a sample cabin crew job description and person specification.

Sample Cabin Crew Job Description
Members of the cabin crew are required to provide exceptional customer service before, during, and after the flight. In addition to this, they are responsible for the safety of themselves, the safety of the other crew members and most importantly, the safety of the passengers. Cabin crew are trained to a very high standard to deal with emergency situations and to also administer first aid when necessary.

Cabin crew will carry out several pre-flight checks, which include assessing all safety equipment and ensuring that the aisles and safety routes are clear from obstructions. They will then welcome on board the passengers and conduct a roll call once all luggage is safely stored away and secured.

Following pre-flight safety briefings, cabin crew will serve refreshments to passengers as well as offer duty free goods and services. All the while, they will have to deal with any passenger complaints, as well as deal with any other issues as and when they arise during the flight.

Qualities of Cabin Crew
While the role will vary between airlines, there are of course identifiable attributes that any strong member of a cabin crew should have. See below for a breakdown of the qualities you need in order to be an effective cabin crew member.

Safety-Conscious Attitude
You will be responsible for the safety of the passengers, so you will need to work in an organised and safe manner. You will also need the ability to learn and retain substantial amounts of safety-related information, procedures, and training. This is what airlines consider to be the most important attribute.

Flexibility
Cabin crew need to be very flexible in order to meet the demands and expectations of the role. Although you will receive your flying roster a few weeks before your scheduled flights, it is important that your diary is kept free to meet it. You may also be required to be on standby and be available to fly at short notice to cover sickness, delays, or cancellations.

Calm Approach and Ability to Work Under Pressure
Despite the perceived glamour of the role, cabin crews work in extremely pressurised situations – and we're not talking about the

altitude! Indeed, passengers can sometimes be very difficult to deal with, and you will need to maintain a calm demeanour always. You will need the ability to deal with complaints effectively while delivering key elements of the role at the same time.

Teamwork Skills
Cabin crew very rarely work with the same people each day. You will find that you work with a large amount of different people during your career, as cabin crew teams vary one day to the next. Therefore, you must have the ability to work with everyone, regardless of their gender, background, age, sexual orientation or religious beliefs.

Pride in Appearance
It goes without saying, but you must be capable of looking after yourself and taking a pride in your appearance. Some airlines will place more emphasis on this attribute than others.

Ability to Follow Procedures
Cabin crew must be able to work unsupervised and follow procedures religiously. Safety is paramount to the role and you will be expected to follow your training to the letter. You will have many rules and procedures to absorb during your training, so an ability to learn and retain a large amount of job-related information is absolutely necessary.

Excellent Customer Service Skills
Air cabin crew staff must have exceptional customer service skills. The competition within the airline industry is extremely fierce, so each airline is competing for every passenger. Of course, one of the most crucial elements of customer satisfaction is the level of service a passenger receives from the airline cabin crew staff. If an airline can get this part right, passengers will not only come back to them in the future, they will also recommend them to other would be passengers. Therefore, when recruiting, airlines will place special emphasis on this attribute.

Organisational Skills
Cabin crew staff must be organised both in their personal lives and their work lives. You will need to keep an organised diary to make sure you are available to meet your flying roster and you will also have to work in an organised manner before, during, and after the flight. You will have checklists to follow pre-flight and you will have certain procedures to follow during the flight. Being organised is all part and parcel of being a competent cabin crew member; it's the whole job, basically.

Numerical Competence

Cabin crew need to be competent in the use of basic arithmetic. During the flight you will need to work with money when selling duty free goods and refreshments. You will also have to have an understanding of currency rates and conversions. Whilst you do not need to be a mathematician to become cabin crew, you should have a good basic understanding of addition, subtraction, multiplication and division.

Being a Role Model for the Airline

This attribute is very similar to customer service skills. The airline wants you to paint them in the best possible light. Therefore, how you behave whilst at work (as well as whilst away from work) is very important.

Excellent Communication Skills

Cabin crew must be able to communicate with the following groups of people:

- Cockpit crew;

- Passengers;

- Other cabin crew team members;

- Airport staff and representatives.

Of course, there will be other people you will have to communicate with during your career, but the above four groups are the main people they have contact with during their day-to-day duties.

So, your communication skills must be excellent. Let's assume that there's a safety issue with the aircraft during the flight and you are required to communicate a safety message to the passengers using the public address (PA) system.

It is essential that you remain calm and communicate the message in a confident and concise manner. If the passengers detect any hint of stress or concern in your voice, they will become agitated.

Of course, there are many other qualities required to become cabin crew, although the above key attributes form the basis of the role. Before you attend the assessments and interview, make sure you learn them, understand them, and be ready to provide evidence of where you have already performed each one in a previous role.

Let's now look at what the cabin crew interview involves.

About the Cabin Crew Interview

During the selection process for becoming cabin crew you will have to undertake at least one interview. This will usually form part of the main assessment day; however, many airlines will also invite you back for a further second interview if you pass the assessment day. The questions in this guide will help you prepare for both sets of interviews and I would urge you to use the same preparation strategy for each interview. In this section we will look at the cabin crew interview and what it involves.

The cabin crew selection panel are highly experienced in being able to determine who are the right people for the job. Therefore, it is vitally important that you prepare well for this stage. The interview panel will normally consist of 2-3 people, with one person being a senior member of the cabin crew training team for that particular airline. There may also me a member of the human resources department sitting on the panel to ensure the interview is conducted in a fair manner.

In order to pass the interview, you will need to provide the selection panel with evidence of where you meet the assessable qualities. Although we will be covering the scoring criteria in the next section of the guide, you need to have the word 'EVIDENCE' at the forefront of your mind before you start your preparation.

In order to score highly during the interview, you need to come up with examples of where you have already demonstrated the key assessable qualities in a previous job or career. If you do this, you will be more likely to succeed during the interview.

The interview panel will be assessing you on the following key areas:

- Your knowledge of the airline you are applying to join;
- Your knowledge of the role of cabin crew;
- What qualities and expertise you can bring to the role;
- The experiences you have that match the assessable qualities;
- Your personal appearance and presentation;
- Your communication skills;
- Your levels of confidence;
- Whether you meet the qualities discussed in the previous section

of this guide.

So, in order to prepare fully for the above assessable areas, you need to direct your pre-interview preparation on the following key areas:

Research

Research, in terms of the role you are applying for and the particular airline you are hoping to join, is essential. During the interview, you are likely to be asked questions relating to the following areas:

- **What you know about the role of a cabin crew member.**
  You should study the role of air cabin crew in detail and think carefully about what it involves. You should also think about the positive sides of the job and also the negatives.

- **The reasons for applying and why you want to join this particular airline.**
  This is important because many applicants simply want to become cabin crew and they do not care which airline it is with. My advice is to ensure that you have a good reason for wanting to join their airline. My motto has always been:

AIRLINE FIRST, CABIN CREW SECOND!

- **What you know about their airline.**
  The most effective way to find out this information is to go to the website of the airline you wish to join. From the website you will be able to find out as much information as possible about what they do, where they fly to and from and also what their values are. In order to help you, here is a checklist of things you need to learn:

Airline Research Topics Checklist

Research Topic	Done?
Who are the senior airline executives and the CEO?	
What aircraft do they operate?	
Where do they fly to and from?	
What are the main services offered?	
Have they won any awards?	
What is their customer charter?	
How do they protect the environment? NOTE: this is sometimes called corporate responsibility.	
What are the special services or special assistance do they offer passengers?	
How many people work for the airline?	
What is the airlines history and heritage?	
Where is the airlines head office located?	

What is new and current within the airline?

Who, if anyone, does the airline sponsor?

What was their latest Twitter post?

What was their latest Facebook post?

The above checklist is an excellent starting point to help you get your research of the airline underway.

- **How you deal with specific situations in your working life and what you learn from them.**
  This is of particular importance and one area that may take you some time to prepare for. This is essentially where you will provide the panel with evidence of your previous experiences; such as, when you have provided excellent customer service, when you have dealt with a customer complaint and also when you have remained calm in a difficult and distressing situation.

When responding to situational interview questions use the **S.T.A.R method** for constructing your responses. Here's an explanation of what it means:

When constructing your responses to the situational questions within this guide, create them using the following format:

S – Situation
Start off by explaining what the situation was and who was involved.

T – Task
Now move on and tell the panel what the task was that you were required to carry out or complete.

A – Action
Then tell the interview panel what action you took and also what action other people took when trying to complete the task.

R – Result
Finish off by telling the panel what the result was following your actions and the actions of the other people involved in the situation. Always try to ensure that the result is a positive one!

If you follow the above method for creating your responses to situational interview questions then your responses will be formulaic, concise and in a logical sequence. This will help you to gain higher scores in the assessable area of effective communication.

- **Challenges faced by the airline.**
  This can be a tricky one to answer; however, just by typing in the words "challenges faced by the airline industry" in to any one of the search engines you will be able to formulate you own views on this subject. To give you an idea of the different challenges at the time of writing, here are some thoughts:

  1. **The environmental impact of the airline industry and an airline's carbon footprint.**
  This is a challenge simply because the demand for air traffic is increasing and is set to continue. With more and more people wanting to fly it is a challenge for airlines to meet their targets.

  2. **The competition within the industry.**
  The competition is becoming fiercer with more airlines offering flights at cheaper prices. Attracting and retaining customers is getting harder. However, by offering customer excellent customer services they are far more likely to return and use the airline again in the future. This is how cabin crew can help the airline meet this challenge.

  3. **The rising cost of fuel.**
  With the rising cost of fuel, it is difficult for airlines to keep their costs down without passing on the added expense to their passengers.

  Of course, the above 3 challenges are not the only ones facing the airline industry, but they are a good starting point.

- **Your own personal qualities and attributes.**

  In order to prepare for question based around this topic, think carefully about the role of cabin crew and also the qualities required to carry out the role competently. It is important that you have these qualities and attributes and be able to demonstrate them at interview.

- **Your strengths and weaknesses.**

  Only you will know what these are; however, the following are good strengths to have when applying for this type of job:

  - Resilience and confidence;

  - Flexibility;

  - Caring nature and attitude;

  - Excellent team working skills;

  - Empathy and understanding;

  - Good communication skills;

  - Personal pride in appearance.

In terms of weaknesses, we all have them and anyone who says otherwise is not being honest. However, be careful what weaknesses you discuss. This is a good weakness to give during the cabin crew interview:

"My weakness is that I detest lateness and on occasions in the past I have been known to be quite blunt and to tell people my thoughts whenever they are late for a meeting or appointment that we have pre-arranged. Because I am never late myself, I expect this of other people and my comments have sometimes been taken the wrong way. However, I am learning that not everyone has high standards in relation to punctuality and I try not to say anything to them."

The above response is quite a good one as it demonstrates to the panel that you are never late, something which is crucial to the role of cabin crew. Whatever weakness you decide to give, make sure you tell the panel that you are taking steps to improve on your weak areas.

- **Team-working skills**

The interview panel will most certainly want to hear evidence of where you have worked effectively as part of a small team. Cabin crew are required to work with other team members to achieve a common goal. That goal is essentially to get the passengers to their destination on time whilst ensuring their safety and providing excellent customer service. Before you go to the interview make sure that you are capable of providing examples of where you have worked effectively as part of a team. Here is a list of just some of the qualities required to work as an effective team member:

- Good communicator;

- Good listening skills;

- Understanding of others;

- Able to focus on the end goal;

- Being adaptable and flexible;

- Supporting other team members;

- Being aware of yours and the other team members strengths and weaknesses;

- Hardworking and focused;

- Professional and conscientious;

- Open to feedback.

Before you go to the cabin crew interview, you should learn and understand the above list of teamworking qualities.

- **Respect and diversity**
  As cabin crew you will be required to work with and interact with people from all walks of life. It is absolutely crucial that you are capable of working with anyone, regardless of their age, sex, religious beliefs, background, sexual orientation, disabilities or otherwise.

Let's now take a look at a number of sample interview questions and responses to help you prepare.

Sample Cabin Crew Interview Questions and Answers

Question Number 1:

Why do you want to become a cabin crew member?

You will, most probably, have already answered this question when completing the application form. If this is the case, have a look at your application form response prior to the interview to make sure you give an alternative answer and also that you do not contradict yourself the second time around.

When answering this question, concentrate on covering the following elements:

- The main reason why – your ambition;

- The suitability of your personal qualities and attributes;

- The positive aspects of the role – variety, flexibility, working with others, etc;

- Helping others/Customer care, etc.

We have provided you with a sample response to this type of question.

Once you have read our response, use it to construct your own using a blank sheet of paper.

Sample Response

"This is something that I have always wanted to do. Ever since I flew on holiday as a child, I have aspired to become a member of a cabin crew team.

Although I enjoy my current job, I would now like a career that is more challenging, varied and exciting.

I believe my own personal qualities would suit the role of a cabin crew member and I get great satisfaction from working in a team environment, where everybody is working towards the same goal.

I understand that delivering a high level of service to the customer is a priority in this industry, and this is something that I would enjoy doing."

Key Areas to Consider

The main reason for wanting to become a cabin crew member:

- The positive aspects of the job;

- Working in a team environment;

- Providing a high standard of customer care.

Question Number 2:

Why do you want to work for our airline?

Once again, you may have already answered this question during the application form stage. If this is the case, remember to check your answer first before attending the interview.

When answering this question, you must be positive about their airline. The main reason for the panel asking this question is that they want to know you have researched them thoroughly, and that you are serious about wanting to join them. Many candidates apply for many different airlines just because they want to become a cabin crew member. Wanting to join their particular airline is just as important as wanting to become a cabin crew member.

When answering this type of question, try to cover the following areas:

- Their reputation (providing it is positive);

- The quality of their product;

- The airlines ambitions and achievements;

- What they stand for.

Now, take a look at the sample response that follows before creating your own using a blank sheet of paper.

Sample Response

"Prior to attending the selection process, I researched a number of different airlines before deciding to apply for yours. I was impressed by the quality of service the airline offers and I already know that it has an excellent reputation. Your customer service standards are high and the quality of training all cabin crew members receive is exceptional.

Having spoken to some of your existing employees, all of them were very happy in their work and stated that you are a very good employer. You are an exciting airline that has achieved much to date and I like the fact that you are always looking for innovative ways to improve and develop.

I would like to work for an airline that cares about its customers, which you do. If the customer is happy and their experience of flying with you is a good one, they are likely to come back again.

I would love to be a part of this team and believe the qualities I have will help it to continue to move forward and stay ahead of its competitors."

Key Areas to Consider:

- The airline's reputation;

- The quality of their product and what they stand for;

- The airline's ambitions and achievements.

Question Number 3:

What makes you better than the next candidate and, therefore, why should we offer you the position?

This is another opportunity for you to sell yourself. This is quite a common question during interviews and the way you approach it should be in a positive manner.

The question is designed to assess your confidence and determine the type of qualities you have. Don't fall into the trap of answering this question in the same way that most people do.

Many people will reply with a response along the following line:

"I am the best person for the job because this is something that I've always wanted to do. I am a hard worker who is enthusiastic and determined to be successful."

This type of response is not factual or unique in content. Try to focus your response on the job and how best you match it. The airline wants to know that they'll look back in a years' time, and think that they are glad they employed you.

Take a look at our sample response before constructing your own using a blank sheet of paper.

Sample Response

"I have researched both the role that I am applying for, and your airline. Looking at the required skills of the role and the type of person you are looking for, I believe I am the best person for the job.

I have a proven track record in delivering a high level of customer service and have experience in dealing with customer complaints. I have been on a number of training courses before and always ensure that I put in the required amount of work to successfully pass them to a high standard.

I am a confident and reliable person who works very well in a team environment. In my previous role as a restaurant manager, I often had to work to tight schedules and always remained calm when under pressure.

Finally, my personal circumstances are extremely flexible and, having studied the role of a cabin crew member, I understand the obligations and requirements in terms of availability. If successful, I promise that I won't let you down and I will work hard to make sure that I live up to expectations of the airline."

Key Areas to Consider:

- Your previous experience and how it relates to the role;

- Be positive, confident and upbeat in your response;

- Cover the key qualities and attributes and match them with your own experience.

Question Number 4:

What are your weaknesses and what do you need to work on?

This is a classic interview question and can be quite difficult to answer for many people.

Those people who say they have no weaknesses are not telling the truth. We all have areas that we can improve on, but you need to be careful what you disclose when responding to this type of question.

For example, if you tell the panel that you are an awful time keeper you might as well leave the interview there and then! They will admire your honesty, but the role requires people who are punctual and are not going to be late for work.

The best way to prepare for this type of question is to write down all your weaknesses. Once you have done that, pick one that you can turn into a positive. Look at the sample response that follows and see how we have turned the weakness around to our advantage.

Once you have read the response, use a blank sheet of paper to prepare your own response based on your own circumstances.

Sample Response

"That's a difficult question to answer but I am aware of a weakness that I have. I tend to set myself high standards both personally and professionally.

The problem is, I sometimes expect it from other people, too. For example, I find it difficult to accept it when people are late for an appointment that we have agreed.

In those situations, I need to learn to let it go over my head and just accept that everybody is different."

Key Areas to Consider:

- Be honest, but don't talk about any weaknesses you may have that are in relation to the job description;

- Turn your weakness into a positive;

- Say that you are working on your weakness;

- If you really cannot think of a weakness, tell them about one that you used to have.

Question Number 5:

Describe a situation at work where you have had to be flexible.

Part of the cabin crew's role is to be flexible.

Part of the essential criteria for becoming a cabin crew member is that you are flexible. This means that you are flexible in terms of the roster and your availability.

In order for the airline to operate effectively, it needs people who do not want to work a normal 9-5 jobs. You may have to be at the airport for 3am to prepare for your flight at 5am. Are you flexible enough to do this?

Many cabin crew staff say that the most frustrating aspect of their job is the instability of the life and the roster changes. Obviously, the airline wants to know that this is not going to be a problem for you. Therefore, when responding to this type of question, you need to provide an example where you have already demonstrated commitment and flexibility to a previous or current role.

Read the sample response we have provided before using a blank sheet of paper to create your own response.

Sample Response

"Whilst working in my current role as a hairdresser, I was asked by my employer to work late every Saturday evening. The reason for this was that several clients could only make appointments between 6pm and 8pm on Saturday evenings. Although I usually go out on a Saturday night, I decided to agree to the additional hours. The salon was doing well and was beginning to get a very good reputation. I wanted to help the salon provide a high level of service to its customers and understood that if I didn't work late on those evenings they would lose the custom.

Fortunately, 2 months on, another member of the team has volunteered to help me cover the Saturday evenings, so I now only have to work every other Saturday.

I fully understand that cabin crew members need to be flexible in terms of their roster and working hours. My personal life would allow for this and I believe it is a small sacrifice to pay for such a rewarding career. I can be relied upon to be flexible when required."

Key Areas to Consider:

- Demonstrate that your personal circumstances allow for flexibility;

- Provide an example where you have gone out of your way to help your employer. Tell them that you understand how important flexible working is to the role of a cabin crew member.

Question Number 6:

What challenges will our airline face in the future and how could you, as a cabin crew member, help us to overcome these?

This type of question serves two main purposes for the panel. The first purpose is that it assesses how much you understand about the airline industry, in terms of its competitiveness.

The second purpose is that it assesses your awareness of how influential cabin crew staff are in their role.

Cabin crew are some of the most important employees of an airline. If passengers have an unpleasant experience during a flight then they are unlikely to return to that airline. There are so many different airlines to choose from and competition is fierce, so staying ahead of the game and providing an exceptional level of service is important. Even if the airline is low budget, in terms of its airfare price, it is still important that the cabin crew staff are friendly, helpful and customer- focused.

Look at our sample response on the following page before constructing your own answer using a blank sheet of paper.

Sample Response

"The airline industry is extremely competitive and the expectations of the customer is always on the increase. People generally want to pay less for their service but still expect a high level of customer care.

In addition to the competitiveness of the modern-day market, there is also the issue of security and the financial implications this has in terms of additional training and advanced security measures. The cost of fuel and salary expenses will continue to increase, which will undoubtedly influence the cost of the product.

Therefore, it is important that cabin crew members provide the highest level of customer service at all times.

Customers are prepared to pay that little bit extra for a high-quality service and the cabin crew staff are responsible for delivering it.

Ensuring the customer is satisfied with the service will mean they are far more likely to come back to the airline time and time again. More importantly however, they will recommend the airline to their friends and relatives."

Key Areas to Consider:

- Competitiveness of the industry, security issues and increased operating costs for the airline;

- High customer expectations and how cabin crew can help deliver this;

- A quality service means customers are far more likely to return and use the service again.

Question Number 7:

Do you think you will find the change of lifestyle it difficult to adapt to, if you are successful in becoming a member of the cabin crew team?

There is only one answer to this question and that is 'No, it will not be difficult to adapt to'.

When answering questions of this nature, tell them that you have researched the role and are fully aware of the implications, including the change of lifestyle it will bring.

Also, remember to touch on the specifics about the change in lifestyle, what it means to you and how you have prepared for it.

Don't be afraid to say that some areas will be a challenge for you, but that you are fully committed and prepared for everything the job presents.

There now follows a sample response. Once again, read it and take any useful ideas from it. Then prepare your own based on your own individual circumstances.

Sample Response

"Although this is something that I have dreamt of doing for many years now, I have still taken the time to consider the lifestyle change and how it will affect me.

Whilst some areas will be challenging, I am 100% confident I will not have any problems adapting. My personal circumstances are such that I can work the roster system comfortably and I am prepared for being away from home for extended periods, as and when required.

I have few personal commitments at home and am fully prepared for the lifestyle change, if I am successful in my application. In fact, I am very much looking forward to the change, as it is something I have wanted for a long time.

I live life to the full and my personality is one that is adaptable to most circumstances."

Key Areas to Consider:

- Smile and be enthusiastic in your response;

- Talk about the change in lifestyle for you and how you have prepared for it. You have thought long and hard about this career and your personal circumstances are suited to the role.

Question Number 8:

How would you deal with somebody in a work situation who you felt was not pulling their weight and working as part of the team?

This type of question can be asked in a variety of formats.

You may be provided with a situation based around somebody not pulling their weight during a flight, or it may be a question asking you to provide an example of where you have dealt with this type of situation in your current or previous role.

Whichever is the case, the question is designed to assess your assertiveness and confidence, whilst being tactful. They are not looking for you to respond in a confrontational manner but, instead, looking for you to approach the person and resolve the issue with the minimum of fuss. To ignore the issue is not an option.

There now follows a response which gives an example of a work situation. Somebody is taking too many breaks and not pulling weight.

Once you have read the example, try to think of any experiences you have where you have had to deal with this type of issue. Then, use a blank sheet of paper to create a response.

Sample Response

"Whilst working in my current role as a waiter for a local restaurant, I was aware of a colleague who was taking more breaks than he was entitled to. Whilst he was taking these additional breaks, the rest of the team would have to cover for the shortfall. Unfortunately, the customer would then suffer as the time it took for them to be served would increase. I decided to approach the person in order to resolve the issue. I walked over to him and asked him in a friendly manner if he would come and help the rest of team serve the customers. I told him that we were busy and that we needed his help. Fortunately, he responded in a positive manner and realised that he was taking advantage of his rest periods. Since then, there has not been an issue.

It is important that the team gets on and works well together. We cannot afford to have confrontational situations and the best way to resolve issues like this is to be honest and tactful."

Key Areas to Consider:

- Do not be confrontational;

- Be tactful in your approach, focusing on the customer as the priority. Effective teamwork is essential;

- Do not ignore the situation, but instead deal with it tactfully.

Question Number 9:

How do you feel about working with people from different cultures and backgrounds?

This is quite a common interview question and one that you need to be prepared for. Respect for diversity is essential to the role of a cabin crew member. You will be working with both colleagues and customers from diverse cultures and backgrounds and, therefore, it is important that you are comfortable with this. We live in a diverse community that brings many positive aspects that we can learn from. When answering the question, you should be aiming to demonstrate that you are totally at ease when working with people from different cultures and backgrounds. You may wish to give an example of this in your response.

Take a look at the following response to this question before using a blank sheet of paper to construct your own answer to this type of question.

Remember to be honest in your reply and only state the facts about your feelings towards people from different cultures. If you are not truthful in your response, you will not be doing yourself, or the airline, any favours.

Sample Response

"I am totally at ease in those situations, in fact I don't even think about it. This has never been a problem for me.

I have a sincere interest in people from different cultures and backgrounds and have learnt many things from them in the past. I would like to think that we can all learn something from everybody, regardless of their culture or background and this is a part of the job that I would look forward to.

There are so many different and exciting things to learn in life and this can only be achieved by meeting, respecting and understanding people from diverse cultures and backgrounds. Teams that are diverse in nature have a better chance of delivering a higher quality of service. If the customer base is diverse, then so should the workforce that delivers the service."

Key Areas to Consider:

- Be honest when answering this type of question;

- Demonstrate that you understand diversity and the benefits this brings to society. Provide examples where appropriate.

Question Number 10:

What is the best example of customer service that you have come across?

The majority of airlines pride themselves on their high level of service. However, some are better than others.

This type of question is designed to see how high your standards are, in relation to customer service. Those people who have a great deal of experience in a customer-focused environment will be able to answer this question with relative ease.

However, those who have little experience in this area will need to spend more time preparing their response.

Try to think of an occasion when you have witnessed an excellent piece of customer service and show that you learned from it. If you are very confident, then you may have an occasion when you, yourself, provided that service. Whatever response you provide, make sure it is unique and stands out.

There now follows a sample response that relates to an individual who went that extra mile to make certain the customer was happy.

Once you have read it, use a blank sheet of paper to create your own.

Sample Response

"Whilst working as a shop assistant in my current role, a member of the public came in to complain to the manager about a pair of football shoes that he had bought for his son's birthday. When his son came to open the present on the morning of his birthday, he noticed that one of the football boots was a larger size than the other. He was supposed to be playing football with his friends that morning and wanted to wear his new boots.

However, due to the shop's mistake, this was not possible. Naturally, the boy was very upset. The manager of the shop was excellent in her approach to dealing with situation. She remained calm throughout and listened to the gentleman very carefully, showing complete empathy for his son's situation. This immediately defused any potential confrontation.

She then told him how sorry she was for the mistake that had happened, and that she would feel exactly the same if it was her own son who it had happened to. She then told the gentleman that she would refund the money in full and give his son a new pair of football boots to the same value as the previous pair.

The man was delighted with her offer. Not only that, she then offered to give the man a further discount of 10% on any future purchase, due to the added inconvenience that was caused by him having to return to the shop to sort out the problem. I learned a lot from the way my manager dealt with this situation. She used exceptional communication skills and remained calm throughout. She then went the extra mile to make the gentleman's journey back to the shop a worthwhile one.

The potential for losing a customer was averted by her actions and I feel sure the man would return to our shop again."

Key Areas to Consider:

- Use an example where somebody has gone the extra mile;

- Remember that part of the role of a cabin crew member is to provide a high level of customer service;

- Tell them what you learned from the experience.

Question Number 11:

What do you think makes a successful cabin crew team?

Part of the role of a cabin crew member is to be a competent and effective team player. The purpose of this question is to assess your knowledge of what a team is and how it operates effectively. Some of the important aspects to remember, when operating as a cabin crew team member, are as follows:

- Gets on well with the rest of the team;

- Offers effective solutions to problem solving;

- Utilises effective listening skills both verbal and non-verbal;

- Makes an effort to involve others;

- Can be adaptable and willing to try others' ideas;

- Gives positive feedback to the rest of the team;

- When things are going wrong, remains positive and enthusiastic.

These are just a few examples of how a member of a team can help contribute in a positive way.

Now, look at the sample response that follows. Then use a blank sheet of paper to construct your own answer.

Sample Response

"There are a number of crucial elements that would make a successful cabin crew team. To begin with, it is important to have several types of people in terms of their personalities, views and opinions. This way you are more likely to get a variety of options and solutions to problems when they arise.

The team members need to be positive, enthusiastic and have the ability to get on with each other. There should be no confrontation between members of the team and an understanding from everyone that they are working together to achieve a common goal of delivering a high-quality service, all the while ensuring the absolute safety of passengers.

Each member of the team should be a competent communicator and be able to listen to other people's ideas and opinions. Flexibility in the team is also important to try new and different ideas when appropriate.

Every team member should provide encouragement and work hard together when the pressure is on. Above all, cabin crew are role models for the airline, and each member of the team should uphold the values of their employer."

Key Areas to Consider:

• Utilise key words in your response;

• Demonstrate that you understand the qualities of an effective team;

• Remember the ultimate aim of delivering a high-quality service and ensuring the safety of all passengers.

Question Number 12:

Have you ever lost your temper?

This is a great interview question and is not easy to answer.

All of us have lost our temper at some point, but you need to be careful as to how much you disclose.

Part of the role of a cabin crew member is to remain calm under pressure and you need to demonstrate this in your response. They do not want to employ people who lose their temper at the slightest hint of confrontation. It is during these times that you will need to use your skills to defuse the conflict.

The question is designed to see how honest you are, and whether you are a naturally aggressive person. It is ok to lose your temper at times during your personal life, but it is not welcome as a cabin crew member.

How would it look if you saw a cabin crew member losing his/her temper during a flight? It would be embarrassing and unprofessional!

Look at the sample response that follows before taking the time to construct your own.

Sample Response

"On the whole I am a calm person and do not become aggressive or confrontational. Whilst it is only natural to be annoyed with people from time to time, I see no point in losing my temper. It is just wasted energy.

I understand that cabin crew staff cannot lose their temper with passengers, it would be highly unprofessional. I appreciate that it must be frustrating at times dealing with difficult passengers, but the way to resolve issues is to remain calm and be patient."

Key Areas to Consider:

- Try to use 'non-confrontational' words and phrases during your response – patience, calm, understanding, etc;

- Demonstrate your understanding of the cabin crew's role and the importance of remaining calm and professional.

Question Number 13:

If you were not successful today would you re-apply?

There is only one answer to this type of question and that is

"Yes, I would".

The question is designed to see how dedicated you are to their particular airline. The important thing to remember, when responding to this type of question, is to mention that you would look to improve on your weak areas for next time.

Determination is the key to success and if you are not accepted the first time, you will work hard to improve for the next time.

Most people, if asked this question think they have failed and are not going to be offered a job. Do not fall into this trap. It is a question that is designed to see how committed you are to join their airline! Be positive in your response.

There now follows a sample response to this type of question. Once you have read it, take the time to construct your own using a blank sheet of paper.

Sample Response

"Yes, I would, most definitely. I have researched many different airlines and this is the one that I would like to join. If I am not successful at this attempt, then I will go away and look for ways to improve. Whilst I would be disappointed, I would not be negative about the situation. One of my qualities is that I can accept, and work on, my weaknesses. If there was the option for feedback, I would take this up and improve on the areas I needed to work on.

However, I would love to be successful at this attempt and do believe that I am ready, now, to become a competent and professional cabin crew member with your airline."

Key Areas to Consider:

- The only plausible answer to this question is 'yes'.

- Be positive about the prospect of not being successful and tell them that you would work on your weaknesses.

- Don't be afraid to be confident in your own abilities.

Question Number 14:

How many times have you called in sick within the last year?

This is an easy question to answer, but one that can do you some damage if you have a poor sickness record.

The ideal answer here is zero days. The airline need people who are reliable.

If a member of the cabin crew calls in sick on the day of their flight, this will cause problems for the airline. They then have to dedicate time and resources to phone around and find somebody else to cover for the sick person.

Genuine sickness cannot be avoided. However, in every job there are people who take advantage of sick leave, which costs employees thousands of pounds every year.

The airline industry is keen to avoid employing people who have a poor sickness record.

There now follows a sample response which is based on an individual who has no record of sickness within the last 12 months.

Sample Response

"I have had no days off sick within the last 12 months.

I am an honest person and would only ever call in sick if I really could not make it to work. I understand that the airline needs to employ reliable people and if a member of the team goes sick, you will need to find somebody else to cover for them."

Key Areas to Consider:

- The fewer days you take off, the better;

- Be aware of the implications for the airline if an employee is constantly calling in sick;

- Genuine sickness cannot be avoided.

In the next section of the guide we will provide you with a useful section that will teach you how to deal with customer complaints, something which you will get asked about during the interview!

Question Number 15:

What would you do if you saw another cabin crew member being rude to a passenger?

Whilst this type of situation is very rare, it has happened and therefore, you should be ready for this type of question. As cabin crew you have a lot of responsibility on your hands and therefore, you should try to resolve the situation yourself. It is important to always apologise when something has gone wrong and in this case, this is what you should do first. Try to soften the situation by perhaps offering the passenger free soft drinks. Do not offer free alcohol as this could make them aggressive as time goes on and they think about the situation they have just found themselves in. Try to avoid escalating the situation to a formal complaint unless the passenger absolutely insists.

Sample Response

"I would try and soften the situation by offering the passengers free drinks or refreshments. I would say to them that I was extremely sorry for what had happened and that I can assure him/her that it won't happen again. I would then assess their response to see whether they wanted to take the matter further.

If they did, then I would speak to my senior member of the cabin crew team. Having said that, reporting a work colleague would be a last resort and I would try my hardest to resolve the situation on my own."

Key areas to consider:

- Be polite and apologise if necessary;

- Reassure the passenger that the situation is not the norm;

- Try to soften the incident by offering free soft drinks;

- If you need to, report the incident to your senior cabin crew member.

Question Number 16:

What would you do if a commercially important passenger complained that another commercially important passenger is snoring too loudly behind him?

The way to deal with this situation is to firstly apologise and then to see if there are any other seats available away from the snoring passenger! You should avoid waking up the snoring passenger as this will just cause embarrassment and a complaint may follow. If there are no seats available anywhere else on the aircraft then you could offer them earplugs or, alternatively, offer to allow them to watch a free film in first class if this is available. This is an unfortunate situation that can only be resolved by having a spare seat available or by offering earplugs.

Sample Response

"I would start off by sympathising and apologising for the situation. I would then look to see if there were any alternative seats available away from the snoring on the aircraft. If there were no seats, then I would offer the passenger earplugs or even the chance to watch a film using headphones."

Key areas to consider:

• Don't wake the snoring passenger unless absolutely necessary.

• Apologise to the offended passenger;

• Look for alternative seating;

• Consider offering earplugs or headphones to watch a film.

Question Number 17:

There are 25 children on your flight, but you only have 12 toys to hand out. how would you deal with this situation?

Most airlines will carry a variety of toys for children of all ages. Naturally, there is only a maximum number that an aircraft can carry; therefore, this type of situation is rare. However, if it does arise then you will need to use your head and a bit of common sense in order to resolve it. You could try to see if there are two children of the same family that perhaps could share one, or alternatively be discreet and only offer toys out to one section of

the aircraft so that the other section does not become aware that toys are being offered out to the children.

Sample Response

"This would be a situation where I would try to use some common sense and see if I could get children from the same family to share one toy.

If it became apparent that I was going to run out of toys then I would probably hand out toys to one section of the aircraft so that the other section was not aware."

Key areas to consider:

- This is a situation that you have little control over;

- Discretion when handing out the toys might work;

- Look for opportunities for children of the same family to share.

Question Number 18:

The aircraft is about to take off but a passenger insists that he must kneel down in order to conduct his prayer due to his religion. what would you do?

Again, this is a very rare situation but one that may occur. If it does happen, it is very difficult to deal with.

Here is Jessica's plan of action for dealing with this situation: *I would personally leave my seat, if safe to do so, and approach the passenger to ask him to return to his seat. I would explain that, whilst I had total respect for his religion, it is for his own safety and the safety of the other passengers that everyone is secured in their seats during take-off. If he refused to sit back and secure himself in his seat then you would need to inform the pilot so that he/she could make a decision. Safety is paramount when flying and it should never be compromised.*

Sample Response

"This is a very difficult and sensitive situation that would need to be handled carefully. The first thing I want to say is that safety is paramount and I understand that the aircraft cannot take-off unless all passengers are secured in their seats. I would probably begin by making an announcement on the overhead speaker that all passengers must remain in their seats with seat belts securely fastened. If this did not work I would then approach the passenger and inform him that he needed to sit back in his seat and secure his seat belt. Whilst speaking to him I would demonstrate respect at all times. If he refused then I would inform the pilot as he or she may decide that the aircraft cannot take-off until all passengers are secured in their seats. Safety would be at the forefront of my mind at all times."

Key areas to consider:

- This is a sensitive situation that will require you to show respect;

- Do not neglect safety on any occasion whilst working as a cabin crew member;

- All passengers must be secured in their seats prior to take-off.

Question Number 19:

Are you – or have you been – applying to other airlines?

The important thing to remember here is that honesty is key. Whilst it would be preferable for you to only apply to the one airline, most people apply to more than one at any one time. The key to answering this question is to make your response a positive one.

Sample Response

"I need to be honest and say that yes I have applied to other airlines. I am very keen to become a cabin crew member; however, I have been careful in the ones that I have selected. My first choice would be this airline and the reasons for that are because, during my research, I have been very impressed with the professionalism and the level of service you offer your passengers. Your airline has the best reputation out of all the ones I have applied to join. I have found that one of the benefits of applying to join a number of different airlines is that you get to see which ones are the best, and this one certainly stands out as the most attractive."

Key areas to consider:

•   It is preferable to apply to just the one airline;

•   If you are applying to more than one airline, turn your response in to a positive situation by telling them why theirs is the best!

Question Number 20:

Tell us about your hobbies.

Whilst this is an easy question to answer you should consider how some of your hobbies may come across. Good hobbies to have are sports, fitness, travelling, languages and culture and music. If you love partying and going to nightclubs then keep this to yourself! The interview panel want people who are grounded and who have a flexible life which can fit in around your busy work schedule as cabin crew.

Sample Response

"I am quite a grounded person but I do have a few hobbies. I love keeping fit and active and I attend the gym a few times a week. I also enjoy traveling and love being away from home. I think it makes you appreciate your home life when you do return after being away from home for a few weeks. When

I travel I enjoy learning about the different cultures and I am also currently learning a new language. When I am not at work I enjoy spending time with my family who are very supportive of my aspiration to become cabin crew."

Key areas to consider:

- A hobby can say a lot about you;

- Think carefully about how your hobbies will portray you to the interview panel;

- Hobbies that involve fitness and health are positive.

Question Number 21:

Do you like children?

If you don't like children then don't become cabin crew! As you are aware, thousands of children fly on holiday each year with their parents. You should therefore like children and be able to work in an environment where there may be a few screaming kids on board.

Sample Response

"I love children and I am very comfortable being around them. I understand that cabin crew must work in an environment where there will undoubtedly be children. Often, those children may be tired and restless and it will be my job to attend to any problems and also make sure they don't disturb other passengers or accidently activate the life jackets."

Key areas to consider:

- It is important that you like children;

- Remember that cabin crew need to have a caring nature and youshould be comfortable attending to them;

- On-board children can be naughty or mischievous and you may have to deal with this kind of situation.

Question Number 22

What can you tell us about our airline?

It is vital that you carry out lots of preparation in relation to airline research before you attend the cabin crew interview. If you don't, you will fail. I recommend that you concentrate on the following key facts:

- The airline's routes;

- Customer service ethos;

- Growth plans for the future;

- Main competitors;

- Financial performance;

- Recent published news.

If you learn these key areas then you will be fully prepared in relation to airline research and knowledge. You will probably be able to find all this information on the website of the airline you are applying to join. The following sample response is in relation to British Airways (info is correct at the time of writing.)

Sample Response

"During my research I learnt a tremendous amount about your airline. You now fly to over 600 destinations worldwide through the franchise, codeshare and oneworld partners from countries such as Albania through to Zimbabwe. From your own website customers can book not only flights to these destinations but they can also book holidays, hire cars, hotels and different experience packages such as skiing holidays. You offer outstanding customer care and you also offer different classes of membership such as the elite executive club service. Your ethos is To Fly, To Serve and the level of customer service is outstanding.

You take corporate responsibility very seriously and at British Airways you want your customers to fly confident that you are acting responsibly to take care of the world that we live in. One Destination is your commitment to grow the airline in a responsible way towards the environment, local communities, partner organisations and individuals.

Each year you publish a report about the progress in this area through the website onedestination.co.uk. Your website recently won the website of the year award and your growth plans are both impressive and responsible. From 14 April, you will be flying three times a week extra from London Gatwick to Colombo, Sri Lanka via Male in the Maldives. In addition to this a new service to Chengdu, the capital of Sichuan Province in China, will begin on 22 September which will include three flights per week from London Heathrow Terminal 5. These two examples are just a small number of your impressive expansion plans.

Your main competitors are many and varied, including Virgin Atlantic and Qatar Airways but it very much depends on the route. A popular route flown is London Heathrow to New York JFK. Many airlines fly that route including Virgin Atlantic, American Airlines and Delta Airlines.

With regards to financial performance the company is achieving its targets during difficult economic times. This is testimony to the way the company operates and the excellent reputation it has.

To conclude, I have been extremely impressed with the professionalism of the airline during my research which has only reaffirmed my wish to join the organisation as cabin crew."

Key areas to consider:

- Focus on learning the key areas of airlines routes, customer service ethos, growth plans, main competitors, financial performance and learning recent published news. If you intend to apply for lots of airlines then this will involve lots of work;

- Don't relay any negative press or news the airline may have received;

- Focus purely on good news stories and positive information;

- Take the time to really learn about the airline as this will greatly increase your chances of success;

- If you can, take the time to learn the customer service ethos off by heart.

Question Number 23

How you would deal with a customer complaint?

Dealing with and resolving a customer complaint is all part and parcel of the cabin crew role. You should have a thorough knowledge and understanding of how to deal with them.

In any industry or profession where a customer is complaining, there are many key areas that the complainant is concerned with:

- They want someone to **listen** to their complaint;

- They want someone to **understand** why they are complaining;

- They want someone to **sort out** their complaint as soon as possible;

- They would like an **apology**;

- They want someone to **explain** what has gone wrong.

Cabin crew members are required to deal with complaints in an efficient and effective manner. When dealing with customer complaints in any form, you will need to follow an action plan. This action plan is explained in detail on the following pages. Whilst I haven't provided you with a specific response to this question, the following information and guidance will help you to answer it sufficiently.

The plan follows a structured format and each area follows on systematically from the other. To begin with, you will listen to the complaint using effective verbal and non-verbal listening skills. Most people associate communication skills primarily with the spoken word. However, these cover several areas. Having the ability to actively listen is a key factor to resolving the complaint successfully. Look at the stages of dealing with complaints before reading each individual section.

1. Listen to the complaint.

2. Apologise and appreciate.

3. Gather information.

4. Provide a solution.

5. Reach an agreement.

6. Take action.

7. Follow up.

Step 1 – Listen to the Complaint
One of the most important factors, when dealing with the complaint, is to listen. Listening effectively can be done in a number of ways. This can be achieved through facial expression, body language, oral confirmation and clarification techniques.

If the passenger is sat down in their chair then you may wish to crouch down to their level. This will alleviate any confrontational body position where you are looking down at the complainant. This will also prevent the need for speaking any louder than necessary. Then, listen to the complaint in full.

Maintain good eye contact throughout, nod, use an interested facial expression and confirm back to the passenger what they have told you. If the passenger begins to shout, becomes aggressive or confrontational, or even starts swearing, then you will have to be assertive in your response and inform them that their language will not be tolerated. Inform them that you want to deal with their complaint quickly and to their satisfaction, but it must be done in a calm manner.

Step 2 – Apologise and Appreciate
Once you have listened to their complaint, you need to apologise and explain that you fully understand how they feel. This will usually have the effect of defusing any confrontation and will make the complainant feel that they are being heard. It is all about establishing a rapport with the passenger and making them feel that their complaint is important. The following is a sample response to a customer's complaint:

"Thank you for taking the time, sir, to explain what the problem is. If the same situation had happened to me I would certainly feel as you do."

In just two sentences, you have made the complainant feel valued and understood. Now you can begin to resolve the issue and you will find it easier to talk to them from now on.

Providing their complaint is genuine, you should now take ownership of the complaint and see it through to a successful resolution. You have listened to their complaint and acknowledged there is an issue. Now move on to establishing the facts, which will give you the tools to create a successful resolution.

Step 3 – Gather Information
When dealing with a complaint as a cabin crew member, the next important stage is to gather as much essential information as possible. The reason

for doing this is that it will allow you to make a more informed judgement about the situation and it will also allow you to take steps to prevent it from happening again.

Complaints take time to deal with and detract you from other important duties. When a member of the team is dealing with a complaint, the rest

of team must make up for the deficit in numbers. Therefore, if the situation that led to the complaint in the first instance can be avoided in the future, this will help the flight to run smoother and allow the cabin crew staff to concentrate on their primary role – providing a high level of customer service and ensuring the safety of all passengers.

When gathering information, concentrate on the following areas:

• What is the complaint in relation to?

• What are the facts of the incident?

• Who was responsible?

• How would the passenger like the problem to be resolved?

Once you have gathered all of the facts, you will then be able to take action to resolve the issue.

Step 4 – Provide a Solution
Coming up with a suitable solution to the customer's complaint can be difficult, especially if they are reluctant to accept any reasonable offering. Therefore, it is important that you remain calm throughout.

Make sure that the solution/s you offer are relevant to the situation and are achievable. If they are not, then do not make the mistake of offering something you cannot deliver. This will just make the situation worse. When providing a solution, ask the customer if your offer is acceptable. For example:

"Would you like me to get you another drink?" or *"Would*

you like me to see if we have an alternative meal?"

By offering different solutions to the complainant you are asking them to make the decision for you, and therefore making your life easier. This way, they will end up getting what they want and, therefore, will be happy with the resolution.

Remember – when dealing with the complaint, never take it personally and never be rude or confrontational.

Step 5 – Reach an Agreement
Once you have offered the solution, make sure you get the complainants approval first. This will prevent them from complaining about the action you are taking to resolve the issue. The most effective method of achieving this is through verbal acknowledgement.

For example:

"Ok sir, to resolve the issue, I will go away and get you another meal. I will make sure that the meal is hot. Is this alright with you?"

Reaching an agreement is important psychologically. The passenger will feel that you are being considerate to their needs and, by reaffirming the solution with them; you are showing them that you have their interests at heart.

Step 6 – Take Action
Plain and simple. Now that you have reached an agreement, get on with task in hand. If it is going to take you a while to take the action agreed upon, you might find it useful to inform the passenger.

"Ok, I will now go and get your meal. This might take me a few minutes, so please bear with me."

Question Number 24:

What are your strengths?

The most effective way to answer this question is to first read the job description and person specification for the job. Once you have done this you will have a good idea of what the main qualities of the role are. You should then answer the question by providing strengths that match the main qualities of the role. This will ensure that you get the highest scores possible for this question. To begin with let's take a look at some of the main qualities required to become cabin crew:

- Effective communicator;

- Team worker;

- Flexible and approachable;

- Customer service orientated;

- Professional;

- Adaptable.

Now look at the following response to this question which perfectly matches these qualities.

Sample Response

"To begin with, I am an excellent communicator and I am able to deal with people from diverse backgrounds comfortable and proficiently. I really enjoy working with other people and I have a happy disposition and a caring nature. Another of my strengths is that I have a flexible approach to work and life in general and I am always highly professional in a work-related situation. Finally, I am adaptable and can be relied upon to work very hard for any organisation."

Key areas to consider:

- Get a copy of the job description and match the key qualities in your response;

- Use positive keywords and phrases in your response that match the main qualities required in the role.

Question 25:

Where would you like to be in 5 years' time?

This is a relatively easy question to answer. The question is designed to assess how long you intend to stay with the airline and what you want to have achieved during that time. Anyone who says they hope to have moved on from the airline they are applying for will not pass the interview. The airline will be investing plenty of time, money and resources in to your development and therefore, they will want to see a return from their investment.

Look at the following response to this question.

Sample Response

"I would like to be working for your airline as a competent member of the team and someone is respected as a hard worker and an integral part of the cabin crew staff. In 5 years' time I would want to be fully trained and highly experienced in the role having gained plenty of experience by learning from other people within the organisation. I am also a keen person and if the chance arises I would hope to be working towards promotion within the company."

Key areas to consider:

- The airline is investing lots of time and money in to your training. You should want to still be with them in 5 years' time;

- Be positive in your responses and if you are keen on promotion, don't be afraid to say so.

Question 26:

Do you prefer working with other people or on your own?

In order to become cabin crew, you will need to have excellent team working skills. Having said that, you will also need to have an ability to work on your own, unsupervised. The correct answer to this question is to inform the interview panel that you prefer to work with others as part of a team, but conversely you are very comfortable working on your own if required. Look at the following response to this question.

Sample Response

"I am very much a team player and love working with people. I am at my happiest when working with other people and when working in a role that involves helping others and delivering an excellent service. Having said that, I am also very comfortable working on my own unsupervised. I can be relied upon to carry out a job or task diligently and to a high standard without the need to be constantly checked."

Key areas to consider:

- Cabin crew work as part of a team with many other members of the airline staff, such as pilots, co-pilots, ground crew, cleaning staff and other members of the organisation. Teamwork is very much part of the role.

Question 27:

What is the most challenging situation you have ever faced?

This question is designed to assess how you react to tough situations in your life. As cabin crew you will be responsible for taking control in emergency situations; there can be nothing more harrowing than having to deal with an emergency situation on-board an aircraft. It will be your job to remain calm in these types of situations and reassure the passengers that everything will be fine and that they need to follow your instructions. Could you do that?

Take a look at the following response to this question which clearly demonstrates the candidate's ability to react calmly to tough situations and resolve them.

Sample Response

"One evening I was sat at home watching television when I heard my next-door neighbours smoke alarm sounding. This is not an unusual occurrence as she is always setting off the alarm whilst cooking. However, on this occasion, something was different as the alarm did not normally sound so late at night. I got up out of my chair and went to see if she was OK. She is a vulnerable, elderly lady and I always look out for her whenever possible. When I arrived next door, I peered through the window and noticed my neighbour sat asleep on the chair in the front room. Wisps of smoke were coming from kitchen so I knew that she was in trouble. I immediately ran back into my house and dialled 999 calmly. I asked for the Fire Service and the Ambulance Service and explained that a person was stuck inside the house with a fire burning in the kitchen. I provided the call operator as much information as possible including landmarks close to our road to make it easier for the Fire Service to find.

As soon as I got off the phone I immediately went around the back of my house to climb over the fence. Mrs Watson, my neighbour, usually leaves her back door unlocked until she goes to bed. I climbed over the fence and tried the door handle. Thankfully the door opened. I entered into the kitchen and turned off the gas heat which was burning dried up soup. I then ran to the front room, woke up Mrs Watson and carried her carefully through the front door, as this was the nearest exit. I then sat Mrs Watson down on the pavement outside and placed my coat around her. It wasn't long before the Fire Service arrived and they took over from them on in. I gave them all of the details relating to the incident and informed them of my actions when in the kitchen."

Key areas to consider:

- Try to provide a situation that was challenging and difficult;

- During your response demonstrate how you managed to stay calm during the situation and try to come up with a positive outcome following your actions.

Question 28:

Do you have any experience of working as a team member?

The ability to work effectively in a team is an extremely important aspect of the cabin crew role. Not only will you be spending a great deal of time with other members of the cabin crew team, you will also depend on your colleagues during potentially stressful incidents and situations. Therefore, it is important that you can demonstrate you have the ability to work as an effective team member.

When responding to this type of question, try to think of occasions when you have been part of a team and achieved a common goal. It is important that you give EVIDENCE of where you have already worked as part of a team in a work situation.

Maybe you are already involved in team sports playing hockey or football? You may also find that you have experience of working as a team member through work. If you have no or very little experience of working as a team member then try to get some before you apply to the airline. After all, teamwork is an important aspect of the role.

Now take a look at the following sample response.

Sample Response

"Yes, I have many years' experience of working in a team environment. To begin with, I have been playing hockey for my local team for the last 3 years. We worked really hard together improving our skills over the course of last season and we managed to win the league.

I am also very much involved in teamwork in my current job. I work as a nurse at the local hospital and in order for the ward to function correctly we must work effectively as a team. My job is to check all of the patients at the beginning of my shift and also make sure that we have enough medical supplies to last the duration. It is then my responsibility to inform the ward sister that the checks have been carried out. She will then obtain more supplies if we need them.

We have to work very closely together for many hours and we all pull together whenever the going gets tough. I enjoy working in a team environment and feel comfortable whilst working under pressure. I would have no problems working as part of a team in my role as cabin crew if I am successful."

Key areas to consider:

- It is important that you provide EVIDENCE of your ability to work as part of a team;

- Before you attend the interview have an understanding of what teamwork is, what it involves and the qualities each team member should possess.

Question 29:

Tell me about a time when you changed how you did something in response to feedback from someone else?

When working as cabin crew you will need to have the ability to listen to, and respond to, feedback from senior members of the team. You should also possess the maturity to admit when you get things wrong and take steps to improve wherever possible. There are always new procedures to learn whilst working as cabin crew and you will receive appraisals on a yearly basis from your superiors. How to structure your response:

Here is a good response to this question.

Sample Response

"During my last appraisal, my line manager identified that I needed to improve in a specific area. I work as a call handler for a large independent communications company. Part of my role involves answering a specific number of calls per hour. If I do not reach my target then this does not allow the company to meet its standards. I found that I was falling behind on the number of calls answered and this was identified during the appraisal. I needed to develop my skills in the manner in which I handled the call. My line manager played back a number of recorded calls that I had dealt with and it was apparent that I was taking too long speaking to the customer about issues that were irrelevant to the call itself. Because I am conscientious and caring person I found myself asking the customer how they were and what kind of day they were having. I was spending too much time on delivering a high-quality service to the customer as opposed to working through the call as fast as possible so that I could answer the next one.

Despite the customers being more than pleased with level of customer care, this approach was not helping the company and therefore I needed to change my approach. I immediately took on-board the comments of my line manager and also took up the offer of development and call handling training. After the training, which took two weeks to complete, I was meeting my targets with ease. This in turn helped the company to reach its call handling targets."

Key areas to consider:

- How you respond to feedback is very important. Try to give a good example where you improved following feedback in a work-related situation.

Question 30:

How would you deal with an unruly customer?

This question can come in two forms, but they're asking similar things. If it's the former, then you need to imagine the scenario. If it's the latter, and you've dealt with an unruly customer in the past, then you'll need to remind yourself of how you behaved.

Whatever the case, bear in mind that there's a correct way to answer this question. Focus on how you defused the situation. In particular, consider if any of the following apply:

- You weren't judgemental towards the customer;

- You carefully considered the situation to figure out what the problem was;

- You showed that you wanted to help them as much as you could;

- You tried to see things from the customer's perspective;

- You took decisive action to remedy the situation.

These are all things that interviewers are looking for, and behaviour that would be expected of you in a situation like this. Therefore, make sure you demonstrate that you can ask in the correct manner.

Sample response

"Fortunately, I have had to deal with unruly customers in past jobs, so I would apply this experience to any similar scenarios faced while in the air. In fact, during my time as a member of bar staff at a student pub, dealing with rowdy/angry patrons became quite the regular occurrence!

As a result, I became adept at spotting the causes of such situations. For example, as protocol dictates, I would stop serving anyone deemed to be 'too drunk'. While this did result in some ill-feeling being amongst those refused, I believe that overall it prevented more trouble than it caused.

While alcohol is not the only cause of unruliness, the same thinking can be applied while working within a cabin crew. During flights, it is probably necessary to be extra vigilant in this regard due to the lack of bouncers to resolve conflicts.

In any case, working to prevent unruly behaviour is just as important as responding to the situations themselves.

Of course, it is impossible to prevent every instance of such behaviour, so a plan of action is needed. Of course, the safety of everyone on board remains the top priority."

Asking Questions at the End of the Interview

Once the interview is over you may be given the opportunity to ask the panel a couple of questions yourself. It is bad practice to not have any questions prepared, so make sure you have two ready in preparation. Personally, I would avoid asking any more than two or three questions. You should remember that the interview panel are busy and that they have

other people to interview. I advise that you ask insightful questions that put you across in a positive manner. Here are three great questions to ask the panel:

Q1. Whilst I am waiting to find out if I am successful or not, is there any further literature of information you can recommend I study to further enhance my knowledge of the company?

This question is great because it shows that you are keen, eager and hungry for more information.

Q2. What is the airlines approach to the training and development of its staff?

This is a good question because it shows that you understand how important training and development is.

Q3. How long would you expect someone to stay in this position before being considered for an internal promotion?

This is a good question because it demonstrates that you are keen to progress but also that you intend staying with the airline for a long period of time.

The Very End of the Interview

Once the interview is over you may be given the opportunity to say a final few words. If this is the case, try saying something like:

"Thank you for inviting me along to the interview today, I have thoroughly enjoyed it. I wanted to say that if I am successful I can assure you that I will provide great customer service to your passengers and will work hard to achieve the high standards that the airline sets. Thank you for your time."

A Few Final Words

The sample interview questions supplied in this section will help you to prepare fully for the cabin crew interview. As already stated, we cannot guarantee that they will come up at your interview, but we hope they cover every eventuality. When preparing for the cabin crew interview work hard, learn as much as you can about the airline and have examples of where you meet each of the qualities required to carry out the role. If you follow this advice then you will be far greater prepared than the vast majority of candidates. Finally, the website www.cabincrew.com has a very useful forum where you can learn more about the interview from people who have already attended it.

Airline Contact Details

Within this section of the guide we have provided airline contact details to make it easier for you to research and apply.

Most airlines provide recruitment information through their websites. When researching the role of both a cabin crew member and the airline, your first port of call should be the website. This will provide you with plenty of up-to-date information about the airline, its products and service, possible future developments and how they operate.

Take a piece of paper and a pen, and then spend some time studying the website of your chosen airline. Write down any information that will help you during your application.

You will also find that many airlines allow you to apply online through their online application form. If this is the case, remember to print off your completed form before submitting it. You will need to refer to it prior to the assessment centre.

Make sure to check that you meet the minimum requirements, of the airline you wish to apply for, before submitting your application form – many of them vary.

While there are hundreds of available airlines, see below for a list of the most common ones as well as their website details.

AIR TANKER
www.airtanker.co.uk

BMI
www.bmiregional.com

BRITISH AIRWAYS
www.britishairways.com

CITY FLYER
www.cityflyerjobs.com

EMIRATES
www.emiratesgroupcareers.com

EASYJET
www.easyjet.com

FLYBE
www.flybe.com

THOMSON
www.tuijobsuk.co.uk

SMALL PLANET
www.smallplanet.aero

OSM AVIATION
www.osmaviation.com/personnel/jobs

NORWEGIAN
www.norwegian.com

GULF AIR
www.gulfaircareers.com

JET2
www.jet2.com

QANTAS
www.qantas.com.au/travel/airlines/careers/global/en

THOMAS COOK
www.thomascook.com

VIRGIN ATLANTIC
careersuk.virgin-atlantic.com

AIR NEW ZEALAND
www.airnewzealand.co.uk/london-based-flight-attendants

FOR AN OVERVIEW OF THE ENTIRE CABIN CREW SELECTION PROCESS SEE OUR OTHER GUIDE:

HOW TO BECOME A CABIN CREW

This guide will tell you how to complete the cabin crew application form, how to prepare for the assessment centre and also how to pass the cabin crew interview!

Gain instant access to over 11 hours of interactive content with our online training course.

For more information go to:
www.CabinCrewCourses.com

Get Access To

FREE

Psychometric
Tests

www.PsychometricTestsOnline.co.uk

13920594R00047

Printed in Great Britain
by Amazon